MW00935868

for bright + beautiful

HYMNS TO THE BELOVED *Gorcen Ann*

POEMS

Such joy

by

'u connect again

Ana Ramana

love alway

Ana

Copyright 2014 by Ana Ramana

All Rights Reserved

ISBN: 978-1500945237   Paperback

Front Cover Image:
from *Madonna with Child and Two Angels*
by Fra Filippo Lippi, circa 1465

Used by permission.

Other books by Ana Ramana:

The Back Door

Taf

Duet with Hummingbird

The Boy Who Would Be Sage

www.anaramana.com
ana@anacallan.com

DEDICATION

for you, beloved reader

Contents

III. SHIVA: The Fire

IV. MAGDALENE AND JESUS: A Love Story

VII. THE GOLDEN QUESTION: Who Am I?

VIII. FREEDOM: Swimming Into Blossom

IX. FOR YOU: Poems To Illuminate Your Heart

INTRODUCTION

These poems were born out of extraordinary grace
bestowed on the poet. In July 2000, while walking
in her native Ireland, Ana Ramana was struck in
the skull by lumber, which flew off a speeding truck.
What ensued was a profound near-death experience
and years of recovery, during which the blow to the
head cracked open the lid of repressed childhood
memories of severe physical and sexual trauma. Ana
is convinced that she was given this 'second' life
in order to heal the wounds of the first. For seven
years, she left the world and dived inside, learning
to embrace each smithereen of memory still held in
the body, to hold it up to the light, and transmute
each wound into love.

Eventually Ana saw clearly that there was no
perpetrator to point a finger at, how violence begets
violence, how even the most cruel of tyrants is
looking for love in some misguided way. She saw, as
she had been shown when she died, that the entire
world is unfolding in utter perfection, down to the
most obscure detail. In truth, she unlearned all she
had previously believed, surrendering to but utterly
trusting in this divine mystery called life.

The sole truth that emerged from that long dark
night was that every single breath arises out of
love; that the planet, existence, consciousness
is permeated with it; that we humans are

embodiments of love, just as every rock, feather, swirl of smoke is. The poet's healing (making whole again) could never have happened without the miracle of a true teacher, who appeared just when she needed him. As an awakened being, Devaji was intimate with the divine, but also human and male. As mentor, spiritual guide and meditation teacher, he gently, truly guided Ana through the dark morass of her past, the rubble of her history, into the light of love.

Although Ana was raised Catholic, she came to see how no religion or dogma has all the answers, how truth is free of doctrine, conviction. The many sages alluded to in this book are manifestations of the divine who have touched the poet intimately. If they share a path, it is the path of the Mystic.

The poems herein are a celebration of human passions, seen from the light of one healed woman, and an offering of that great and complex gift back to the original source. The poet hopes they will transcend spiritual affiliation and reach the heart of each reader.

RAMANA MAHARSHI (whom the poet calls variously, Ram, Rama) was an Indian sage and mystic, who spent twenty years in a cave, absorbed in the bliss of being, and only came out to serve others. He remained almost silent for his entire life, sharing a few jewels to guide the spiritual seeker. If he gave the world one word, it would be 'non dual.'

No doctrine, no ritual, just the possibility of seeing how the world is not dualistic but one great emanation of love. He said there are two paths to God: one is pure devotion, surrender. One is Self-Enquiry, the act of questioning every thought, of bringing it back to the source by posing the simple question, Who Am I?

ARUNACHULA is the holy mountain to which Ramana was magnetically drawn as a boy of 16, after he had an experience of the body physically dying and seeing that something endured beyond the flesh. He left his family, school, friends, and with just a few rupees, set off for Arunachula, and never left his sacred mountain for the rest of his days. An ashram evolved around him for people were enthralled by and drawn to his light and humble wisdom.

ARUNACHULA is said to be the physical manifestation of SHIVA, Hindu God of Creation and Destruction, who slays the ego with a clean, uncompromising swath. PARVATI is his consort. ARUNACHULA is not a visual knockout, like, say, the Himalayas, and yet its sacredness is uncontested. As Ramana himself said,"God is the most humble of all."

JESUS is said to be the Son of God who came to save the world by suffering for its sins.

Both Ramana and Jesus have been compared for their taking on of others' pain, one poet calling it 'vicarious penance." Jesus died on the cross, threaded with thorns; Ramana died of bone cancer, without any medication.

MARY MAGDALENE was the consort and disciple of Jesus.

PRADAKSHINA is the circumambulation of Arunachula, an act that is popular especially on the full moon when one's sins can be expiated.

BRAHMAN is the totality of gods, The One into which all notions of God and Other are subsumed.

DARSHAN is being in the physical presence of a Master.

PRASAD is a food offering to the gods.

Hymn To The Beloved

Stars hover
like kisses
over our house.
A cow lows
in the distance,
his bell tinkling
the night air.
A praying mantis
flew into my face
this evening
before prayer,
his green and tender
body my skin's blessing.
Oh Lord, I could
build a shrine to you
every day in my heart,
I could fill it with
moon and sun, with
the lemon butterflies
that milk our path
to the sea, with spume
of wave on rock, tall
cactus mad with bloom,
I could fill it with pebbles
and sand from my shoe, with
a dart of lizard and peak of
jack rabbits's ears.

I could add
the languorous sway of ferns
in our courtyard, the breeze-ruffled
curtains in my room. I could take
the luminous, rain-freshened
desert, and set that there too, add
the fan of vulture and hawk wings,
the glorious palmful of spider
as he traces a love pact on the
wall.

Oh God,
I could fill each left space
with kisses and a horse's call,
with the slow swank of donkey
in a clearing. I could conjure
a brimming altar of dawn sky,
each mountain's sinuous fall
and rise, a dozen setting moons,
and still it would not begin
to praise.

Let me at least spend
my days trying. Let me fail you
a thousand ways. Let me breathe
one more, Lord, of your ravishing
days and I will tell lovers and children
and the bird at twilight
of your deepest secrets.

I.

RAMANA: FALLING IN LOVE

One

When His love flowers through,
I am hopeless but to be His lover
arms fondling every tress
of his creation – the lid
of garbage cans is Him,
plastic flowers I have to kiss,
helpless to resist His
Heaven-scented beauty,
tongue, heart, lips
licking tendril clouds
used-up leaves, mislaid
rings for keys, all of it
is He, He whispers
through the reeds,
In every single thing,
find me. And I do,
stroking, rocking,
holding lost parts
of his body, fear
and loss and greed,
bullets, blame,
disease, all of it
His holy kingdom,
of which I am a vassal
and a fool, stupid
with love for Him,
smitten with the dream
of His entire Being.

How It Started

Ramana sliced Ana's heart wide open
and a million hummingbirds came
clattering out, the sky teeming
with ruby and moss and loose
feathers. Ana just could not
pull herself together, she knew
that she was dead, and look,
just look! what lived now
in her stead, the vivid flow
of nectar and wings shimmer
shimmering and deeply drinking
every vibrant thing in.

Seduction

His eyes are not eyes.
They are the essence
of perfect god light, streaming
past all of creation,
merged with eternity.

They are married to The Secret,
God's exquisite kiss.
They are the chalice
that can speak
a thousand languages
in one whisper of silence.

They are galaxies of liquid,
disembodied.

They are the fire
that can free you
and transport you
into Love's ecstatic bliss.

Marry Me, He Said

And I shall wear a white dress
of lace and bird froth and a
veil of air, and a ring on my hand
of twined grasses twelve shades of moss,
and I shall sing thy name to the heavens,
my lover, my spouse, my man,

my healer, my deepest pleasure,
my master, my holiest Ram.

I shall sing your beauty forever
from this heart that was born
of you, and bear all of your joys
and sorrows in our love –

I DO !! I DO! I DOOOOO!!!!

in our love that is pure and true
and your silence, o darling Rama,
hums through my fingers and limbs

as I lift them up to our mountain,
in the wildest, Ana Ram Ramana hymn.

Freeing The Clouds

If Ramana's heart is the sky,
which it is to me,
then moon and sun
are his eyes,
and together

they would dazzle,
if not
blind us
with their fierce light,

so in his ever-kindness,
he doles out his *darshan*
in sweet packages

our hearts can imbibe
all day long
and all night.

Ramana Appears To Me As A Wild Animal

As a sleek mountain lion traversing the road,
jewel eyes drinking me in, or me winking back
at the vast fountain of his love, ferocious
and true, and we feast on each other
until both are subsumed in the fire
that rips through all separation,
until all rules of me and you
are shredded, eaten alive,
both stalker and prey
leaving nothing but holiest grace,
nothing but cinders, dying
into the light
in its wake.

All

All I wanted was a hand to hold
through the forest, through
the dark woods
but Rama offered his Heart,
all rubies and jewels and spaciousness,
all humans and time and wounded creatures
illumined in his love

until he fine tuned my fingers,
fused them into his,
into One Palm uplifted

– a liquid charm –

dripping back
to its sparkling origin.

Pradakshina With The King

For a while Ramana let me be his walking stick
as he moved around his sacred hill,
o god, he could lean on me so beautifully
and he did, each step of his a miraculous
rhythm to which my being tuned and

when he sat, I tilted back and watched
the sky nourishing its clouds, his
palm all the while upon my head,
which in his care had become
a crown of jewels and lotuses,

rising up to Heaven's crest
above us and raining softly
down on man and wood
and mountain

all of it God's bounty
offered from his One Heart,
out of which all 'i' had
been carved, and hewn

now to bark and dust,
a bent branch hollowed
just enough to be allowed
to carry him, gleaming
and hallowed by his handsome
and o unspeakably tender hand.

Poetry

Ramana's heart is liquid gold
streaming from the mountain
into the open bowl
of my head.

My mouth is full of flowers
he has sown for me –
buttercup and tulip,
daisy and wild rose

and every time I swallow,
a petal unfolds and dives
down the green stalk
of my throat

until my heart unfolds
into an infinite bouquet
– in all its shades –
at last swimming
into blossom.

When I Die

I'd like Ramana to be painted on my lips,
his name graven into the shivering fish of my
mouth,
each tooth an alphabet of his,
each letter sending home
a gift of love so true,
the body rendered useless,
skin just memory of a you that never existed,
a life's dream,

and the funeral:
a steady, yielding, unrelenting kiss
that drifts simply
into emptiness,
into endlessness.

II.

HOLY MOUNTAIN: THE PROPOSAL

Because It Is Leap Year

I ask Holy Mountain to marry me.

"Will you take me as your lawful wife?"

"You are already taken," she replies,
offering a bouquet of jasmine.

"I marry you now
to your own flowering."

I ask Shiva if I can be his bride
and he comes down from his perch
with a garland of beads, saying,

"Wear these and see whose bride
you have always been.

I now wed you to Truth."

And darling Rama, I don't have to ask.
We are lovers, forever entwined,
twin grapes on a luscious vine
now growing inside my heart

which folds into Him,
The One Spouse to whom
all vows are offered.

And he tucks the moon in my mouth
and the sun in my heart

and my pockets sprout
with a thousand stars.

And the wind is a ring on my finger
that whispers,

"You are a feather plucked
from the wing of Brahman.

Float out on the dream
as long as you need

but always remember,
I wed you to Love."

– February 29, 2008

August Moon

Moon comes hungering over the tree tips,
warm and rosy from her visit to Holy Mountain,
lusty with love for him, shining and sleek,
her round heart without edges, all shimmering
she, as she lifts her face high to the heavens
in spasms of ecstasy, unbridled, but bride
to His Highness, toasty and gold, before
slipping beneath his dark garments, shy
lover magnificent, already whole.

You Are My Heart

O Arunachula!

You are the flower of my Being.

You are the melody that soars
through lifetimes
in this wild, illusive dream.

But you are not elusive.
You are the steady font of love
that flows in endless waves of grace
through every strand of us.

Strand us now into lustrous jewels
that make music to enchant you.

Will you receive the petals
that we scatter at your feet?

Let us turn to you
in humble gratitude
as you deliver us
of our impurities

as you draw us slowly,
surely, passionately
back to The Absolute.

First Star Over Arunachula

And when I woke,
I strolled down to the ditch
where wild clover and puffball sprigs
and daisies made their kingdom.

Showered in a jewelry of mist
and dew, I knelt to sniff it
and then I found
amidst the purple flowers
my Crown Prince,

a slithery thread
of silver and lime green
breathing like a fish

erect as royalty,
arms settled on a leaf
with uncommon grace,

his tail a lengthy swish
curled at the tip like lace,

his tongue a lily pad
of vivid pink,

his eyes two steady beads
that slowly blinked
and drank me in.

I'd spent the month
dripping kisses on every frog
I found in my shower,
drain and sink

but they were only preludes
for this King In Waiting

– presiding over lily,
mint and twig –
granting me a visit

to a realm I was familiar with
back when fairies and human
were lovers and kin.

I opened the petals of my heart
to him in delight at the surprise
of a mountain god
where I least expected

and when I most needed him.

Surrender

The golden glow of Holy Mountain
folds all children into her ample arms,
dried petals and leaves
of our imagined stories all stored
in her boundless bounty, each
bittersweet sensation drop into
the one priceless pearl, leaving
only beauty and the blinding
light of Truth, that we belong
and always have to He Who
Abides in the Heart of All
Beings, our saving grace,
our brilliant star, the moon
that cools the raging fire,
luring towards surrender,
relieving us until we are
seduced into the lap
of pure and untouched love.

Today I Married A Mountain

Essence of Aruna flowers
strewn astride my crown

in a river bath of petals
gliding slowly down my hair

colors catching in cream
and yellow strands

green leaves easing
onto nipple, elbow, hips

joy of cool shimmer liquid
cleansing from the outside in

eyes on fire
as my spouse Holy Mountain
gazes down

serenely smiling at His nude
woman swaying in the grass

crickets, toads and dogs
singing happily along

at this marriage feast
of heart to holy heart,

twinned stars erupting
through the clouds

lighting up the dark.

Truth

Arunachula is the crown jewel of mountains
but she doesn't dress herself up,
even though from her innermost heart
issue sashes of all colors.

Every cracked rock, stalk of wheat,
every wild dog she receives as her own,
tender mother, as she offers the balm
of deep peace from her secret
unvarnished caves.

Her shawl is stained with waste and defecation
and her suitors, as they walk, thread
their troubles round her waist,
yet she doesn't flinch or resist, kind lover,
for God is the most humble of all.

III.

SHIVA: THE FIRE

Creation

For the joy of his beloved,
Shiva sundered his flesh.

In one thunderous move,
He created two.

Linga of Light
Become Half Man,

Half Woman, to show
how all separation is

illusion, how he himself
is the full fusion

is the single source

of all that seems to
breathe and move.

One cleft flesh he laid
before us to teach

how each tributary
is not off course

and will flow
or shudder

eventually

back to its true
origin.

My Lord of the Shimmering Limbs

My Candlelit Lord

My Lord of Divine Composition

You are the bird in my hand
when the hand is crushed.

You are my freedom,
my truth,
you're my undefiled love.

All the bells in my heart
and the chains in my gut
are clamoring for you,
for one life-giving touch.

My love is a flood of long nights,
of wild tears and blood.

It is a fire, a fury of flowers
in bud, erupting
in blossom through
the pores of my skin.

Where o where
can I hide now,

My Lord of the Mountain,

My One Lord of White Light?

Ash

Shiva is coming for me
with his cloak of gold
and wildfire.

He is stoking the flame
of every last place
that still believes in desire
and heeds it.

He is raising the heat
with magnificent force,

a fury of jewels singed
and torched under
the crunch of his foot.

thoughts flailing
in electric waves
of burn and scorch.

The perfect torture
– o rapturous dance –

all longing and need
washed clean at last
by the storm of tears

all trace of me
finally ground into
blissful dust, leaving

his unrivaled gift
laid out in the ash:

the exquisite signature
of freedom.

Shiva's Gift

Everything dies
on the path to Arunachula

every thought
and desire
every notion of time

Everything burns
on the path to Shasta

all the old habits
attachments and greeds

Everything melts
in the face of the Master:
God shaped into
mountain for the grace
of all humans

Everything lost
on the trail
is forsaken gladly

so nothing
is felt apart

so nothing
but Love
remains

to spill into
the One Waiting Heart.

IV.

MAGDALENE AND JESUS:

A LOVE STORY

Good Friday

At dawn,
she lifts her arms
towards the sun
and falls suddenly
forward.

At dusk,
she sips three
palms of water,
shivering.

Nightfall, and
she's chasing
moon up the hill,
frantic for a trace
of him.

The air is silver
dust, her shawl
brimful
of stars.

His body
may be *awol*
but he cannot
be too far

for death is only
camouflage, as life,
a film of flesh so thin

she can almost feel
his heartbeat pulsing
through her flimsy skin

can almost taste
the lumber of his arms
around her waist

hauling her into
the wood and grit
and mist of him

woundless
soundless
lyric of the heavens

Holy Saturday

She misses him
as if she now had only
half a heart

or just one lung:
she can still breathe,
delicately

as if her heart
were an instrument
with strings plucked

at God's mad whim:
thousands of them
pulling, tugging

hauling up a fishing
net of sorrows

of wild, inexplicable
love to which

she's married,
lover or not

flesh or rot,

she lives always
inside
the body of God.

Easter Sunday

O Magdalene,
did roses sprout from your feet
as he slid into the tomb
of your womaning?

Did all the birds sing
as he chanted a hymn
to rhyme with your
heartbeat? As one hand

bloomed on the secret
sky of your chest,
the other burrowing
down under?

Did God nest
in the wilds of your hair
as you rose and he dipped
into you there

on that cushion of moss,
making liquid of fingers
and air?

Who named it rapture.
this vine of skin and
moisture, this dream
of yoked limbs, this
edible feast of warm
flesh, who named it
love well made
knew well
of what he spoke

and he spoke
only of silence.

Them

He is a guest in her heart.
She is his lady in waiting.

He is a red translucence.
She, a quivering bow.

He is gaunt silhouette.
She, sun-infused shadow.

Easter Monday

All night she lies next to his tomb.

Seraphim swim inside her head,
which has become a womb
that seems to hold the world –

sky and birds deer and words,
everything but him –

And then the vision:

the garden is a shroud
of light beaming from
his chest. She reaches
out her finger twigs,

which almost meet his,
risen now in prayer, visible
yet not quite there, and the singing

Noli me tangere. Touch me not.

Her breasts a fury of desire,
torched in the lavish fire
of his heart

as she takes back her limbs,
ravished,

and lurches down the hill,
cherry blossom wedded
to her lips.

Relief

It wasn't easy being his,
knowing how he loved women
and they loved him

and yet when he folded
into her, when he ate
every aspect of her
face, all starvation

disappeared as she bathed
in the waterfall of hair
under his arm, as she sipped
and bit, as he took her tail
of nose into his own mouth's
cave, they melted in the endless
tide that they rose out of,

the one flow that beholds
and devours separation,

in the ecstatic unison of god,
who whispered through the birds
at sundown, through his own
unbridled heart,

love doesn't hoard.

Magnolia and Grapes

The buds still closed
but not as tight

pink tongues
in sweet repose

pale fingers molded
into prayer.

Russet and sea green grapes
not yet picked

and laid
on the table

only his heaped hands
could fit.

Hallowed

The kitchen is a shaft
of light.

She slices bread
and pours from
the urn of milk
into a pitcher,

which could be his mouth,
so creamy silk,

or hers,
head tilted back
to receive

exactly what,
she isn't sure,

the room her hands
loose crumbs

are one great blur,

the ache of parts
becoming whole

through her tears.

Orbitless

The moon is hollow.

She never knew
she could punch
her fist straight through

or perhaps it's her
who doesn't exist,

freed of her past,
her future, leaving

gorgeous formless
fusion.

Wednesday

The air is colder now.

Wine still lingering in the cup.
fish picked at, set aside.

Her home is made of bones.

There is a hole in the sky:
he is alive inside it.

Wind billowing
in the water
its endless
dress

as she comes inside
to wait

gratefully

for death.

Mellow

The tulips open in a froth
of red, which is his heart
blossoming, which is her

silence settling into cream
and crimson petals, with a
dusting of black seeds
spilling onto table

and her tongue as she leans
into their heaven center,
o godstruck twin,

and revels
in their secret
golden yellow.

V.

HEAVENLY MOTHERS

Ammachi

It was just a sign
in a window: *Indian Saint
coming to town.* Her face
seemed kind, inviting
and though I'd shelved
off God for years, somehow
I found myself
in the great hall, lined
up behind a hundred
people, inching slowly
towards the altar
where she beamed.

Robed in orange,
her earthy eyes
gleamed, sparking
hints of Paradise.

I waited as she leaned
towards each visitor,
showering grace on
every one. And then
there she was, her eyes
gazing deeply as if
she could see
through me.

A hand
reached out to touch
mine and suddenly
she was hugging me.

Oh, the bounty
of her love
flooded every cell.

She leaned close
and whispered
in my ear, *you are*
so beautiful inside
and out. I thought
she had mistaken
me for someone else

but no, her light
smiled directly on me,
wounded creature,
drinking of Heaven's
fountain, now slowly,
surely healing.

Our Lady

You were so far away,
a sylph in the clouds
I couldn't reach. Too
perfect to approach
properly.

And still I prayed
to you in the Pro
Cathedral, lit
a candle, bowed,
two days before

the lumber soared
through air and
smashed into my skull
when death became
my intimate.

How could I trust
your grace when
you had taken away
all that I once
held precious?

Years it took
to embrace the
sidelong blessing,
the opportunity

you gave to shed
completely
that dark past?

For ages,
your purity
scared me,
unworthiness
behaving like
a bully.

How could your distant
form embrace that broken
woman, give her

the hug she craved?
You who seemed
so untouchable,
all I could do
was shove you away

in the back pocket
of my heart
with all those
other unwelcome
memories.

And now,
decades on,
I see how
you reflected
all that time

what I could be

if I gave up
resistance
to my true being,

if I let the light
shine through
and radiate
the beauty
that bore me.

How stubbornly
the ego clung
to its story
of smallness

a crutch that
no longer serves
even her. And now
another of your children
appreciates your
patience and raises
a white flag

and plants a single
lily at your feet,
hoping you will
savor its
unique and grateful
fragrance.

Anandamayi Ma

Like Venkata,
you were always happy.

Mother of Smiles,
they sang to you
as a child.

Gentle, hardworking, obedient,
you knew all that mattered
without learning.

Your only yearning was for God

and oh, how He sang to you too.

O Holy Ma-Ma,
your beauty cannot be measured.

How could your love for all creatures be contained?

You seduced plants with your whispers.

You slid in and out of God-trance.

You lived and died without stain

and we, the flowers in your garden,
blossom for you, unlearning,
page by page, our dark past

so we can flow into the Now
of your heart

melting into the One Faceless Face.

Bhaiji

When he was very ill,
Ma invited him to visit
so he could rest
in her grace and
heal.

Four years he traveled
with her and when
he left, he just
closed his eyes
to find her.

He went to Kashi
to bathe in the holy
waters of the Ganges
but slipped on stone
and fell into the swirling
liquid. Screaming, he

sunk down into the
blackness – the ghost
of death whirling
all around him –

until a pair
of hands slid
beneath his arms
and raised him
like a miracle
up into air.

At that same time,
Ma was miles away
sitting behind a temple.

Her clothes were drenched
so that she had to wring out
the water from her sari.

How close to us they live
and abide – our sacred
masters – assisting us
through every trial,

the sun beam of their love
igniting our lives
always, no matter
how it seems.

Only One

One day, a man arrived
and sat with Ma, imploring
her to help
with his conversion.

He'd been a Christian
and asked which Indian
saint he should bow to.

Ma told him there was
no need, he didn't have
to choose or change

but he was angry.
He knew
what he wanted.

As he took his leave,
his feet stopped at the door
turning round
for one last *darshan*

and found in place
of Ma, the perfect
form of Jesus.

Amma

The Hugging Saint
they call her

and though we've
never met

she swept me up
in a vast embrace

that shook me
to the core

filaments of light
sparking on the air

galaxies of love
so tender

that stars floodlit
my heart

and I, so long
afraid of mothers,

melted and I watched
a flower grow

in that empty place,
abandoned long ago

so every time
she comes to mind

a smile floats
up – a miracle –

and finally,
after that long journey,

I am complete
and perfectly whole.

VI.

RAMANA: ASHRAM DAYS

You Are Always Carried

In the early ashram years,
Ramana's old friend
from his school days
came to see him
and reminisced about
their carefree ways.

So Ramana whispered,
"Let us meet by the tank
at 3 a.m. tomorrow
while everyone is asleep."

And so the pair splashed
and slapped each other
in the water, two joyous
boys cavorting, a swish
of stars at their hips.

For three nights, they met
in secret until
someone heard of this

and soon a charm of boys
lined up at at water's edge

and Ramana, in his grace,
came to them
and lowered his tiny form
into the liquid, heaving
one young man onto his back

and swam all the way across
before easing his precious
package onto land

and then swam back.

For hours, every day,
he conveyed his beloved tribe
from shore to shore

as he does, even now,
his clear hand guiding us
on that tide
that flows towards freedom.

How, I wonder, could we ever
ask for more?

Royal Flush

The Scottish lady wrote
that every evening,
she followed Ramana
as he went on
his evening stroll.

She saw cows straining
at their leash,
unable to contain
their love for He
Who Gave Them All.

Once released,
they raced along
the trail to catch up
with their Beloved.

A charm of dogs and children
ambled in their wake.

And then a deer, monkeys,
half a dozen snakes.

Out of the air,
a thousand swallows
glutted the sky,
so many, they formed
an ink stain
on the horizon.

Vultures too swirled
and dipped to pay
their respect
to His Eminence.

All this, she witnessed
in awe and wonder,
a thunder of kites
spinning round his crown

until the father
of their family
circled round
to Home,

and, as if
in a dream,

the birds melted
back into the trees.

The cows, satisfied,
settled in their stall.

The vultures gave
up flight

and a peace
suffused
the mountain

all now graced
by He Who Is
King Of All.

Ramanapadananda

At the sound of his holy name,
he'd leap in the air, tears
streaming down his cheeks,
a cloud of dust beneath him.

Ramana's true devotee,
helpless but to love him,
to lay his life at Master's feet.

When his work dragged him
back to Madurai, he shipped
gifts almost daily. A jar
of honey, candy dripping
with palmyra juice.
They would arrive
at the ashram just as
Ramana was thinking
of each item.

He traveled far and wide
sharing the beauty of
his sage, placing his
famous portrait on
a chair for all to see,
proclaiming the grace
of the greatest avatar
in history.

Once, singing his Beloved's
praises at Gokarnam,
he fell into a trance
and felt his body to be
exactly that of Bhagavan.

After he came to,
he wrote a letter saying,
"I cannot endure
my torments any more"
and raced back
to the feet of the only
One who mattered.

When the sage asked
why he'd fled a sacred
feast that thousands
were flocking to, he replied,
"You are my Lord Shiva,
I must be at your side."

When the war robbed him
of all he had, he sobbed
to his Master, who said,
"Don't worry. Just surrender
to Him who you adore."

And he did, Ramanapadananda,
He who rejoices at Ramana's feet.

As he thanked Bhagavan
for his darshan, Master replied,

"Who is giving *darshan* to whom?
I say you have given it to me."

Grace

The Maharaja of Mysore arrived
one day at the ashram and pleaded
for a private audience with the sage.

Devotees knew that Ramana
did not favor special cases.
He treated everyone the same.

But Shantammal led
the visitor anyway,
to where Bhagavan
was taking his bath.

Trays of sweets and dainties
were offered as *prasad*
while the Maharaja greeted
his Master,
staring,
then sobbing
and prostrating.

Tears rivered down his face,
so many that they wet
Ramana's feet.

Days later Shantammal
enquired about
the visit.

"Oh, he is a ripe fruit."
Ramana smiled
and with great feeling,
replayed
the scene.

The man had told him,

"they made me
a Maharaja and bound
me to a throne.

For the sin
of being born
a king, I lost
the chance
to sit at your feet

and serve
in your glorious presence."

As he was leaving,
he said,
"I cannot stay here
nor can I come again.

Just these few
moments are mine.
I can only pray
for your grace."

Which Ramana
surely bestowed
on one so humble,
so devoted,

who would imbibe
the gift of his *darshan*
for the rest of his
scripted days.

Natesa Iyer

sitting on a wall
outside the ashram
after he has been banned

but he will not
abandon his Master,
now dead, and hews
close to him as he can.

Natesa Iyer, tired
of being bullied
by the cooks

rolls his anger
out in the grass,
screaming

and finally
gives up and
walks,

forty miles,
before Ramana
appears before him
and smiles,

*How far have you gone
from me?* and floats

like a ghost back
towards Home,
as Natesa meekly
follows

he who rebuked
money, his hands
burning at the touch
of it,

he who made meals
for the hungry
all night long

even as his hands
were shaking, even
as his body ached,
he was living the bid

of the Master and
needed only that.

And then
the moment comes
after Ramana has shown
him he is not the flesh:

He hears his Master
tell him he will soon
be dead, ten days and
counting. Oh yes,

his eyes gleam
with light,
he is ecstatic
to sacrifice the world,
his ears pinned
for the word.

Is Bhagavan coming?
I am coming! and
he is gone.

God's humble
servant finally drawn
back into his light,
leaving no room
for regret or
useless goodbyes.

He and Ramana
now fused into one,
royalty on Heaven's throne.

Surprise!

The English lady was so enthralled
when she saw Ramana's ten line poem,

liquid words from The Master
who was dying,

right arm swollen
and oozing pus

yet carefully writing
word after word,

the lady already
relishing

a formal translation
in homage to the Divine

until Ramana gave her
a wicked smile

and held the page up,
showing off to all

who would look
his new composition:

a god-given recipe
from the hand of light,

inscribed with great care
for laxatives.

Faith

Annamalai Swami took Major Chadwick
for a stroll on Holy Mountain,
and half way up, Chadwick's sandal
strap snapped in half.

Annamalai worried that his friend
could not walk barefoot
but before he could speak,
the Major threw back his head
and bellowed, "Arunachula!
O Arunachula!"

No sooner had his voice
echoed over the hill
than a shepherd appeared.

"What's the matter?"
he asked and once

he knew, he pried
a nail from his shoe
and stitched the sandal
so it felt
like new.

Annamalai watched in awe
as the Major nodded,
"I called out to God
and He came to my aid."

Later, Ramana, hearing
the tale, agreed. "You cried
out to the Lord in full trust,"
he smiled, "and were rewarded."

Devotion

The Dutchman found a photo
of Ramana
and fell in love.

In his small room in Holland,
he sat before it,
meditating on the heart center
waiting for a sign.

For months he sat quietly,
communing with the right side
of his chest
where Ramana said
the true heart resides.

Then late one night,
he heard it.
Come, he said,
my son. And so
he went to Arunachula
and bowed before
the sage.

He sank into a state of bliss
at first, delighted,
but still he was not
satisfied.

*What use is this when
my thoughts are running
wild?* he said.
He prayed
with all his might
for Ramana to quiet
his mind but still
the thoughts crashed
through.

Help me, Master,
he beseeched.
*I cannot bear one thought
that keeps me from you.*

Weeks sailed on
and still he had no peace

until Ramana turned
his gaze on him,
radiating light,
piercing through
the busyness of mind.

The Dutchman wept
in gratitude, relieved at last
and sat for days
in pure untrammeled
stillness.

Weeks after he went home,
Ramana eased out of his flesh
and soared in starlight
streaming across the sky

while the Dutchman sat
in his room in Holland
silent.

For years, he gazed
into the eyes of His Master
held within a frame

and meditated ceaselessly
on Who Am I?

After decades of this solitary
life, he called his friends
inviting them to a party
at his home.

They shared a drink
and idle chat
until the Dutchman stood up
and said, *I am going
to join my Master now*

as his friends watched
him lie down at the feet
of Ramana's picture
and die.

Annamalai Swami

Go to Palakottu,
Ramana told him,
and meditate alone.

Don't even think
of coming back.

Annamalai bowed his head
in reverence and in shock
and lugged his humble heart
to the western edge
of the ashram

and though he missed his Master
like an amputated arm,
though he longed to serve
his Beloved endlessly,
his surrender was so strong,
he turned his passion inward
to find the one source of Love.

Some days Ramana would kindly
come to visit so his boy
was not alone in his devotion
to the truth

until he could look within
and find the Self revealed
to be not separate or apart

but Ramana in residence
as the radiance of his own
perfected heart.

Lovers

Every relationship is communion
with The Beloved.

The bluebird on the flower pot,
the rose next to him,
grass under your feet.
The breeze wafting on
your skin. The man who woos or
wounds you, all of it is him.

A devotee of Ramana wrote many tales
of life with his Master. Then he died.
When Ramana heard, he gathered
every issue of the magazine the man
had scribed on him, and tore out
each page, sewing them into
a binder. "There!" He smiled.
"He always felt his work should
be in a book. Now it is done."

In the presence of such Light,
only Love survives.

After Ramana had sent Annamalai
Swami away, he saw him walking
behind the ashram. "Oh," Ramana
cried. "He always enjoyed the Avial.
Let us fix some for him now."

And he called to Annamalai
to come in from the dark
and eat, as he held a torch
so his beloved boy could
find and savor every last morsel.

Heed the love in the eyes
of whatever you see.
It is him gleaming at you.
The girl singing in the distance,
the train shuffling by,
a spider luring you out
of silence.

Your lover is alive inside you,
bursting with charms. Each breath
is a gift and a prayer. Shine on,
beautiful, beloved creature, embrace
the dream. Be still. Dare to
let him find you.

Homage

Towards the end,
he still offered *darshan*
in the Hall
to help those hungry hearts
who longed for union
with the God of All.

And yet his feebled flesh
shook like a petal
in a storm
and the weight of human pain
caused his head to drop
down to his chest.

He, always composed, erect,
staring into Infinity,
now, with great effort, tried
to raise his head to level.

It was a crucifixion
for those he loved,
bearing all he could
to absolve the sins
of those who loved him.

And then the bondage
on his withered arm
began to seep with
ruby puddles of blood

spreading like a disease
in crimson down
to his wrist, even
his fingers drenched in it.

The women sitting with him wept.
The men looked on in horror

and he, O merciful Sage,
turned his face towards
the torn wound so softly
as if to apologize
for the disturbance.

O God in poignant human form
relieving us.

O God, make us worthy
of He Who Is Most Humble
of All.

Round His Head

There's a thorn on the rug
left over from some roses
I laid out for him, and
for practice, I press it
deep into my skin

and wince. I try again,
more deeply, and it pricks
so that my eyes turn to

liquid, and I recall how
he, on his mountain walks,
would step on thorns

without a thought, dozens
burning into his toes

and heels, remaining
wordless until a man
complained of one wedged

in his sole, and Rama
raised his feet to show
a mess of blood and X's,

splinters arrowing in
all directions, meaningless

since that first time
he bore them all...

VII.

THE GOLDEN QUESTION:

WHO AM I?

Who Am I?

Dip your heart
in the Golden Question
and the ocean of knowing
will yield its nectar.

What has always been you
will disrobe, will unveil
itself so you may marry
your beauty, your singular
truth, so you may become
that one Love that has waited
lifetimes, that has never,
ever abandoned you.

Fall into me, lay down the past,
let your mind be freed of its shackles
so you may shine as that light
– O Illumined One –
your very birthright
for eternity.

Flow

Softly they fold me into me,
these waves.

The moon is a white sheet
in the sky.

I breathe deep and more deeply
until I become the sea, until
I become the air, the sand,
a grain ground into nothing

until I flower into
every single thing.

I have become the sun,
I have fallen into light.
More true is that
the 'i' has simply
taken flight.

The dream world is
a silver sheen of dust
where I used to live
but now the heart has exploded
and wants to give and give
and give itself
to what truly is.

The answer to every question
is the same.
It removes all that separates.
It is everything that seems small
and all that is great.

It is love pure and free
and is undeniably your true nature.

No One

When the mouth closes,
the heart flowers open.

When the eyelids lower,
the whole world explodes
inside like a fire

until it subsides.

When the feet and arms
lay down their chores,
love floods in
and opens the door

to the silence,
to your very own source,

snuffing out all feeling,
all sound,
all perception,
all thought

and what remains
can revel in its own
beauty, its glory.

Rapture

Heart says, I Am.
Mind says, I Am The Body.
Mouth tries to say Silence
but is speechless.

Love says, Me.
In Love says, You.
Pure Love doesn't speak
but fuses two into we

until Truth parts
her lips before
everything blunt
and whispers, whispers

– o sweet seduction –
– one, my Lord, One. –

I AM

a spark from the heart of Ramana,
shattering apart in that first explosion,
falling into the dream, playing
my role but always tenderly
holding a remnant
of the Prince of Peace.

The kiss of Brahman breathing me
as I stumble, then fall in the Mystery.

Always tethered to that one question,
Who Am I?
until all is seen.

My secret self no longer secret,
the original essence now revealed.

Merging back into the whole,
I am nothing
but That

– O Empress of Presence –
eternally.

Now

Beyond the stubborn clutch of this body,
I AM.

Beyond the wild stories, the desiring
mind. Far beyond fear of what's

passed or may come, I AM.

Before these dream lives,
our given names,
those random borders
that hold us in place,
and the running away from,
still I AM.

And who are you?

Will you join me too
in that singular jewel
that abides through
all imaginings, all
ancestors and tribe,
before all notion
of yours and mine
in that perfect,
eternal, unceasing
I?

VIII.

FREEDOM:

SWIMMING INTO BLOSSOM

The Lap of Love

Let me, O God, be most intimate
with my own heart.

Relieve me of the crust congealed
in crevices.

Lure me into the lap of love
where you and I abide as One,
and always have.

Why do I resist?

Who is it hides from her real home?

What dream of me keeps me
from your truth?

Don't let me stray like a wild dog,
gnawing on the bone of illusion.

My one wish is for you.
to fall into your arms, O my Beloved,
to rest in the quiet of your charms.

What is this dream of life
but a chance to die into the light
of your Pure Being?

Let me live as That,
while breath still courses through.

I lay my paws at your lotus feet,
O Holy Master.

One gaze from you and I am free.

I close my eyes now
that I may truly see.

And They Write My Poems

How can these hands be of love?
I asked my Lord each morning.

Sometimes he would make a shawl
of them to hold a bird
or to open a door for someone
passing.

Sometimes he would have them comb
a stranger's length to give him pleasure,
or mold them into claws to scratch
a boy attacking. Sometimes
he would have them be at leisure.

I worried that these hands
were wasted

raising bread to mouth,
glass to lips,
tobacco clutched between
nervous fingers.

But these hands are his,
he told me once
when I least expected.

Lying on my bed,
he gave me such a tender kiss
and stroked my hair

then raised my arms
and folded them
like lost wings coming home

and whispered, *My Dear,*
no matter what you think,
your hands have always
been in prayer.

The Invitation

When the Master calls
and you lay down your arms
and rest open and clear
as the breeze,

He lures you
on the silkiest thread
into His deepest reaches

and you melt into
the lap of God
so soft and kind
and warm, yet

vaster than all
galaxies.

The sweetest rose,
the singing bird,
all language rendered
speechless.

And even the breath,
that precious bridge,
collapses to its knees

until there is only
One Heart

enraptured, love
folded into itself

and it is Heaven
and Home and you've

always belonged
and how could you ever leave

Yet somehow again, you form
eyes and limbs, and the mind,
that stubborn thief,
insists on speaking

But the taste of such grace
lingers, and you carry
into the dream
that sacred gift,
your secret,

emblazoned now
by your perfect lover's kiss.

Vertigo

When it started,
I lay in the grass
and watched the stars
spinning wildly
around me

and I spun
with them.

Standing on a bridge
made me nauseous.

Then it passed.

For years, the world remained steady
while I swirled in circles inside.

Then last week,
it came back,
the mad dizziness.

This time it seemed
a movie revved up
to high speed.

At first, it took
my breath away,
this twirling of images
in vibrant hues.

It longed to suck me into it.

But this time,
I made it my bride
and stayed still.

Let the world spin out
its crazy carnival.

Kaleidoscopes no longer
mesmerize.

I am going
nowhere.

I am the light
with the pictures refracting
off it, the slip-sliding
mirror that once
made me hide.

Nothing can touch the stillness.

Can you taste it now,
pure and eternal,
in every blooming
and dying thing
until even that
disappears?

Like you, I have taken
my seat on his holy throne
of royalty, to rest
in what is unmoving.

Tell me, where else
could we possibly sit?

Choiring

All day long, they sing to me
in a symphony of silver.

Is it a charm of angels
flapping their white wings

or a generous god
come to visit?

They are, I'm sure, celestial beings
making music of my heart.

Every cell is floodlit.

Rainbow hues swirl around the room
though my eyes are not open.

I am the sun wedded
to the moon.

I am the spouse of heavenly realms

and when I think of Ramana,
a trumpet sounds, rising out of
bells and cymbals

at a pitch that soars
far beyond language.

Yet it is poetry
pure and true.

Shiva is a chime
of burnished gold spinning
at my feet.

My crown is humming.

Every single thing is royalty.

Love has become silence,
has become music
and I cannot find anything
separate.

I may as well be dead
yet have never been more alive.

They are singing without cease

and oh delicious god, no one
no one no one is imbibing.

Passion

When they came to slaughter him,
the bull fell to his knees and wept,
great big tears rivering down
his darkened face

and the workers watched in shock
and awe, this creature pleading
for his life, a picture of humility,
and they knew they could not take him.

Instead they sat around his lumpen flesh
in a circle of love, stroking his quaking
head with tender hands, and he looked
into the eyes of each man so wide
openly, and suddenly calm

that every heart melted like sun
kissed butter

and as they led him to a field
where he could gaze at sky
and dandelions, this time
he went willingly towards

the fate we all live and die for:
to rest in pure, exquisite being.

Into Freedom

When Ramana and the angels come for me,
I lie in the grass and loosen
this garment of flesh,
both burden and joy,
that has carried me.

And I am in love with each tender breath,
with each miraculous gift bequeathed
– the bird on the branch,
the broken girl –
it is a perfect tapestry.

The mirage of old stories
rises up in the air
– fireflies merging
into one beam of light.

And now I see that
I have loved one man,
one woman,
one creature,
and they are all me.

When my eyes flow into His,
it is a wedding kiss for eternity.

And as I melt into the stars,
the field is flooded with flowers
blossoming into that delicious, radiant heart.

IX.

FOR YOU: POEMS TO ILLUMINATE

YOUR HEART

Pearl Beyond Price

Tell me, my dearest one,
who were you before the stories,
before you fell into form?

Who are you now?

What worry is it shrouds you
from your truth?

Lure me into your deepest heart
for that is surely where I'll meet you.

Hold up your imagined wounds
to the light.

Let love seep through.

Let it drench you
in the sheer, unsullied beauty
that bore and blossomed you.

Immerse yourself in its golden glow.

Absolve yourself of any darkness.

Unleash the radiant grace
that is your birthright.

Stop at nothing, my loveliest child.

Let your passion for your true self
unfurl the perfect pearl
that is you.

Why keep on roaming,
my sweetest creature,
in the dream world?

Take my hand.

Let true love carry you home.

The Answer Lies Within

Today I am folding everything I perceive
into my heart. Its bounty is enormous.
The wilting larkspur on the altar,
the fire alarm at 3 a.m.,
the brother who spurned me.

Welcome, I say, come on in. There is
room for everyone. To the dead squirrel
on the road, his paw bloodied crimson,
Hello, I say, come home. To the writhing
snake beneath my car, I say, old
friend, don't be a stranger.

And those feelings that bubble up
as I sit are cream rising to the
crest of awareness. I love you,
I say, think what you will,
nothing is being turned from
today.

And the lips on their own
wing up in a smile, a half
moon that feels ready
and ripe for whatever words

are exchanged, the hug offered,
the arm pulled away, oh dear
beauties, you are me, I am you,
I say.

And I bow to the bitter email,
words flung back at me from
my reflection, a brilliant boomerang.

What can I do but prostrate
to the wonder of love seeping
through each creature, mirrors
of light blasting the dark?

Dream The In-Loveness

of your own heart
until you can feel it.

Let your life be That,
a hymn to your blemishless being.

Shine your light like the sun
spreading over the meadow
at dawn, growing brighter.

How far have your trawled?

How long have you sought
The Answer?

How often has the key
to Eternity been laid
at your feet?

Lean now
into the secret.

Open without need.

Embrace the bouquet
of all that's unknown
but know this:

You have always
been free.

Laugh in the face
of what scares you

For he hides
in the sleeve
of your deepest fear.

Don't doubt
that the craving
is him, bearing
intimate gifts
of what is most true.

Give up all
you have believed.

Be Still. Listen
to the love
that is more
exquisite than life.

Heed. Heed now.
He is coming
for you.

Deeply

When you meet someone, think deeply.
It is God who dwells in that body.

— Ramana

Think deeply. How he breathes you,
how he beats your heart.

He moves and sleeps you.
He is eating you
with the fuel of His love.

And when you see another,
it is him beaming at you.

Even if the smile seems like a grimace,
smile back
for God wears many masks.

And if you see a woman crying,
weep with her
or stroke away her tears
for she is a broken part of you
seeking wholeness.

The soldier that you judge,
the sulky child you resist,
the father who ignored you
are all his.

They are lost parts of your self
wanting to come Home
when you truly open to them.

Think deeply. Those differences
are appearance. They arise
out of God, they burn
with that same flame of light
that can never be extinguished.

Make peace with yourself.
Make love of what still wounds you.

Let pain be your ally,
anger your friend

for he too dwells in you
as in your apparent enemy
and will see you through
always to the end.

Harmony

after seeing *A Late Quartet*

The quartet folds into
the cream of the One,
a lyric symphony.

The sad cellist,
the misguided violinist,
nothing can stay separate
as the music rises.

So it is in the dream world:
the mother who didn't know
how to love,
the father who lost his way,
the wandering girl,
her heart broken.

Melt into the melody
as they begin to play.

They must give up
their sad past,
relinquish all sense of other.
These islands have been
lonely long enough.

How else can the celestial
fugue ever happen?

One chord of me against you
and the song of the heavens
is off key.

All sense of knowing
must die
so they can fuse
on the tide of the tune
to great heights
never known in this
mad fantasy of life

so they can play
their part with passion
and love without need

and explode in a starburst
of light

a rare composition
that can rock
the heavens
and make even
the stubborn gods
weep.

Rest

in the haven of your own heart.

Melt in the honey
of your Being.

Feel the creamy warmth
of your essence

gushing through

what you once claimed
to be you.

Give up your claim
on believing,
on doing,

my Beloved. Just Be.

And watch it softly unfurl:

– your birthright –

the pure heaven of Eternity.

For You

Wherever you are is perfect.
Even if you're pushing
into the wind, even if
hailstones lash at your face.
If you've sunk deep
into quicksand, still
consider it grace.

Those voices inside
that speak otherwise,
ignore them.

Let yourself rest.

There's a stream
of crystal water
floating you forward
even if you can't see
it. There is a wisdom
that conjured the way

and it will take you
wherever it is
you are destined to go
or to stay. Trust it.

Have faith. Let love
cast a glow
when it is dark.

You have already
traveled so far
going nowhere.

Listen to your heart.
Can't you hear
it whisper the song
only you know,

that tune that is
your familiar,
the one that sings
your name?

Heed the hints
along the path,
the secret answers
you've always craved.

Be who you are
and be gentle,
be kind to the

worn out
struggling mind.

Let me share
my own secret
with you – if you
believe nothing else,
believe this:

you are already
perfect, exquisitely
whole. Nothing
is lacking.

God only knows
you have tried
to jam up
the holes
you imagined
you carried inside.

Let fresh air
billow through them
like stars igniting
the sky. You

belong right here,
right now – just
as you are.
Please take
my advice and
love the gift

that is unwrapping
itself in your lap
as you sit with
closed eyes.

Open to the beauty
that is alive
everywhere, that
is your true essence.

Please don't despair.
I have come to ask you
to fully imbibe

your magnificence.
Whoever you are,
you are perfect.

Spread your wings,
precious beauty,
and fly.

ACKNOWLEDGMENTS

This book owes its life to many, foremost my beloved Master, Ramana Maharshi. I'm also deeply indebted to my spiritual teacher, Devaji and his wife, Sura, who expertly and lovingly guided me through the fire of the ego's dissolution and lured me more deeply into my True Self.

I can't exclude the beautiful sangha community, with whom I meditate regularly and share monthly retreats. Many of the poems you read here were written during those times of deep silence and communion with the Self.

Endless praise goes to dearest Michael Veys and Julio for their continued support, patience, and love as Hymns To The Beloved gradually evolved. And a huge thank you for the two author photos he took.

There are no words to express my appreciation for the wondrous women's Council who rallied round with heaps of love to support me as I struggled with how to usher my work into the world, honor the silence, and also create a living. Their sage wisdom, advice and encouragement moved me to tears many times. I bow to each of you amazing, generous-hearted women, without whom this book would never have materialized. Particular appreciation goes to my cherished friend and passionate supporter, Lynn Patterson, who offered lavish support at a time when it was most needed. Hugs of supreme gratitude also to the bountiful being of Judy Morgan, as well as to the warm and steady love of Pema Deane, Jude Burns, Caroline Jones, Shanti Joy, and to beautiful Sura, who suggested the Council in the first place.

Immense thank yous too to my beloveds Amrita Brummel Smith and Lily Keller, who championed my work and held a space of love for me from afar.

My delight and thanks to Prem Das Caulley, who spent countless hours conjuring the exquisite gold surround on the book's cover. I am thrilled to have his artistic mastery grace this book.

Aaron Rose too deserves a hug of huge appreciation for his sage advice and masterful design of this book's cover.

And unspeakable gratitude to the holy mountains Arunachula, India, and Mt. Shasta, California, who played their part in this journey of liberation.

It hardly needs to be said that my heart will forever bow to each of the Divine Beings celebrated in these pages. Without their all-embracing love and support, this book would never have found its way into your hands.

And a final hug of gratitude to you too, dear reader. May you find solace, inspiration, or fuel for pondering in these poems and may the light of your divine nature ignite and guide your way.

ABOUT THE AUTHOR

Ana Ramana grew up in Dublin, Ireland and now lives in Mt. Shasta, California. She earned an M.A. in Poetry from Johns Hopkins University. She has published three collections of poems and a novel. Ana is the recipient of multiple awards including The Academy of American Poets Prize and The William Stafford Fellowship. Her work has been anthologized and published worldwide, including The Mountain Path (India), Non Duality Magazine and The Daily Now. She has been the Featured Poet on the websites Poets International; Stillness Speaks; and One The Magazine. Ana has taught at many universities and writing conferences and has lectured on Poetry and Healing at Florida State University Medical School. She has been Writer In Residence at grade and high schools and has worked with the terminally ill and the elderly.

Ana offers intimate workshops and retreats in Spiritual Memoir Writing, Mystic Poetry, and Grief Processing by invitation. If you would like her to tailor a session for your writing or spiritual group, please see her website, anaramana.com, or email her at ana@anacallan.com. You can also find Ana on Facebook and videos of her poetry readings on Youtube. intimaciesoftheheart.wordpress.com features Ana's blog, a series of meditative essays on her encounters with animals and the natural world.

48444606R00096

Made in the USA
Charleston, SC
02 November 2015